Molly's New Toy

Mike Brownlow • Jonatronix

OXFORD
UNIVERSITY PRESS

In this story ...

Max

Tiger

Nok

Molly

Nok woke up late.

Max was playing outside with Tiger.

Nok looked for something to do inside.

Nok went into Molly's bedroom. He looked around. He saw Molly's dolls in their home.

Nok could hear footsteps. They were getting closer.
Nok hid in with the dolls.

Molly came in. She saw Nok.
"A new doll!" she said. "I will call
you Mr Blue."

"You can ride on Mrs Donkey," said Molly.
She trotted Nok around her bedroom.

Max and Tiger came upstairs to play with Nok.
They looked in Max's room but they could not see him.

They looked in Molly's room. They saw Molly playing with Nok and the dolls.
"We must help Nok to escape," said Tiger.

"Could I have that toy?" asked Max, pointing to Nok.
"No!" said Molly. "We are playing. Go away!"

"We need to get Nok back without upsetting Molly," said Max.
"I have a plan," said Tiger.
Max and Tiger shrank.

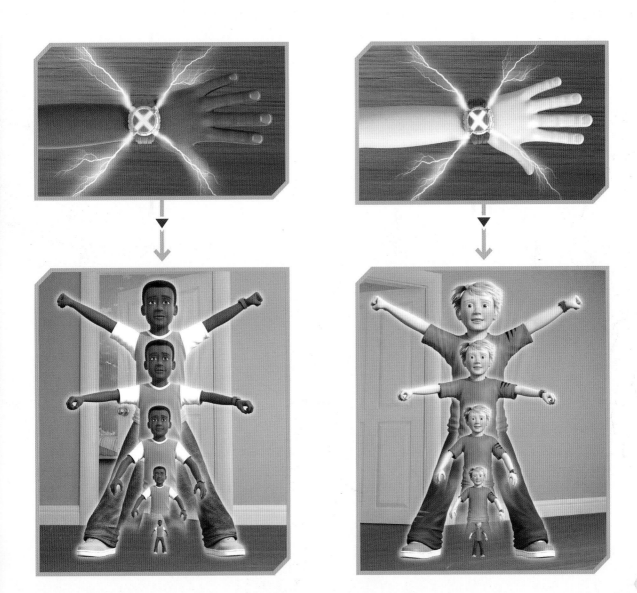

"It's bedtime for dolls," Molly said. "That includes you, Mr Blue."
She did not see Max and Tiger creep in.

Max and Tiger put a new doll in the bed.
"Time to escape!" said Max, whispering
to Nok.

Max, Tiger and Nok crept on their tiptoes out of the room. Then they ran back into Max's bedroom.

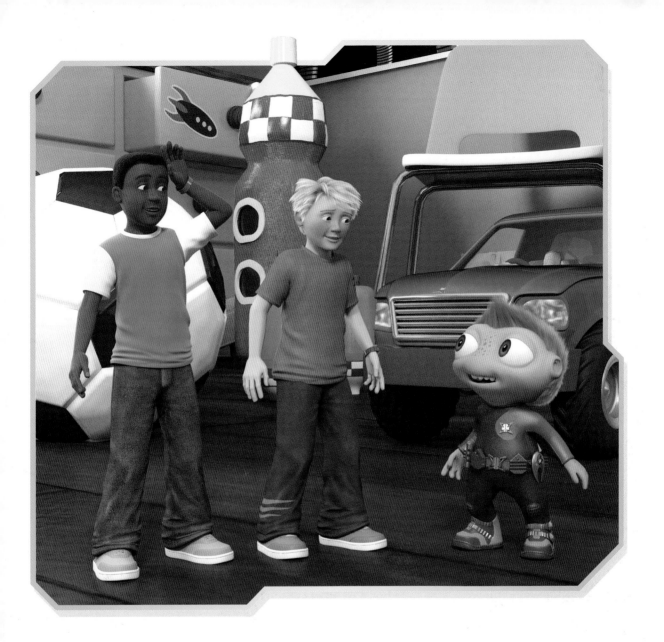

"Phew!" said Max.

"I am glad you got me back," said Nok.

"I prefer playing with toys to being a toy!"

Retell the story

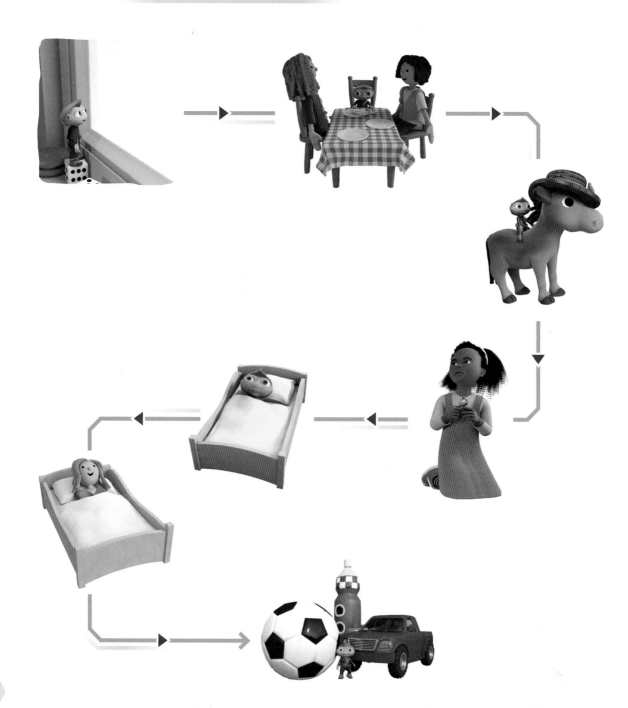